FIRST 50 SONGS
YOU SHOULD PLAY ON THE SAX

ISBN 978-1-5400-0430-7

7777 W. BLUEMOUND RD. P.O. BOX 13819 MILWAUKEE, WI 53213

Visit Hal Leonard Online at
www.halleonard.com

ALL OF ME

Sax

Words and Music by JOHN STEPHENS
and TOBY GAD

ALL YOU NEED IS LOVE

SAX

Words and Music by JOHN LENNON
and PAUL McCARTNEY

AMAZING GRACE

SAX

Traditional American Melody

BAKER STREET

SAX

Words and Music by
GERRY RAFFERTY

BASIN STREET BLUES

SAX

Words and Music by
SPENCER WILLIAMS

(small notes optional)

BEST SONG EVER

SAX

Words and Music by EDWARD DREWETT,
WAYNE HECTOR, JULIAN BUNETTA
and JOHN RYAN

CARNIVAL OF VENICE

SAX

By JULIUS BENEDICT

CIRCLE OF LIFE
from THE LION KING

SAX

Music by ELTON JOHN
Lyrics by TIM RICE

Moderately (with an African beat)

EVERMORE
from BEAUTY AND THE BEAST

SAX

Music by ALAN MENKEN
Lyrics by TIM RICE

DEACON BLUES

Words and Music by WALTER BECKER
and DONALD FAGEN

SAX

Play small notes
2nd time only

FIGHT SONG

SAX

Words and Music by RACHEL PLATTEN
and DAVE BASSETT

FLY ME TO THE MOON
(In Other Words)

SAX

Words and Music by
BART HOWARD

THE FOOL ON THE HILL

Words and Music by JOHN LENNON
and PAUL McCARTNEY

Sax

GOD BLESS AMERICA®

SAX

Words and Music by
IRVING BERLIN

THE GODFATHER
(Love Theme)

from the Paramount Picture THE GODFATHER

By NINO ROTA

SAX

Slowly and expressively

HALLELUJAH

SAX

Words and Music by
LEONARD COHEN

HAPPY

from DESPICABLE ME 2

Words and Music by
PHARRELL WILLIAMS

SAX

HELLO

SAX

Words and Music by
LIONEL RICHIE

Slow Ballad

HELLO, DOLLY!

from HELLO, DOLLY!

Music and Lyric by
JERRY HERMAN

HOW DEEP IS YOUR LOVE

from the Motion Picture SATURDAY NIGHT FEVER

SAX

Words and Music by BARRY GIBB,
ROBIN GIBB and MAURICE GIBB

Moderately

THE HUSTLE

SAX

Words and Music by
VAN McCOY

I WILL ALWAYS LOVE YOU

SAX

Words and Music by
DOLLY PARTON

Moderately slow

small notes optional

IN THE MOOD

Sax

By JOE GARLAND

JUST GIVE ME A REASON

SAX

Words and Music by ALECIA MOORE,
JEFF BHASKER and NATE RUESS

CODA

JUST THE TWO OF US

SAX

Words and Music by RALPH MacDONALD,
WILLIAM SALTER and BILL WITHERS

MAS QUE NADA

SAX

Words and Music by
JORGE BEN

JUST THE WAY YOU ARE

SAX

Words and Music by BRUNO MARS,
ARI LEVINE, PHILIP LAWRENCE,
KHARI CAIN and KHALIL WALTON

LET IT GO
from FROZEN

SAX

Music and Lyrics by KRISTEN ANDERSON-LOPEZ
and ROBERT LOPEZ

Slowly, in 2

MANEATER

SAX

Words and Music by SARA ALLEN,
DARYL HALL and JOHN OATES

Moderately, in 2

MY HEART WILL GO ON
(Love Theme from 'Titanic')
from the Paramount and Twentieth Century Fox Motion Picture TITANIC

SAX

Music by JAMES HORNER
Lyric by WILL JENNINGS

OLD TIME ROCK & ROLL

SAX

Words and Music by GEORGE JACKSON
and THOMAS E. JONES III

(small notes optional)

NIGHT TRAIN

SAX

Words by OSCAR WASHINGTON
and LEWIS C. SIMPKINS
Music by JIMMY FORREST

PETER GUNN
Theme Song from the Television Series

By HENRY MANCINI

SAX

THE PINK PANTHER

from THE PINK PANTHER

By Henry Mancini

Sax

PURE IMAGINATION
from WILLY WONKA AND THE CHOCOLATE FACTORY

SAX

Words and Music by LESLIE BRICUSSE
and ANTHONY NEWLEY

ROAR

SAX

Words and Music by KATY PERRY,
MAX MARTIN, DR. LUKE,
BONNIE McKEE and HENRY WALTER

Moderately

ROLLING IN THE DEEP

SAX

Words and Music by ADELE ADKINS
and PAUL EPWORTH

SATIN DOLL

SAX

By DUKE ELLINGTON

SEE YOU AGAIN

from FURIOUS 7

Words and Music by CAMERON THOMAZ,
CHARLIE PUTH, JUSTIN FRANKS
and ANDREW CEDAR

Sax

SHAKE IT OFF

SAX

Words and Music by TAYLOR SWIFT,
MAX MARTIN and SHELLBACK

SONGBIRD

SAX

By KENNY G

STAND BY ME

SAX

Words and Music by JERRY LEIBER,
MIKE STOLLER and BEN E. KING

Moderately, with a beat

THE STAR-SPANGLED BANNER

Words by FRANCIS SCOTT KEY
Music by JOHN STAFFORD SMITH

Sax

With spirit

STAY WITH ME

SAX

Words and Music by SAM SMITH,
JAMES NAPIER, WILLIAM EDWARD PHILLIPS,
TOM PETTY and JEFF LYNNE

STOMPIN' AT THE SAVOY

By BENNY GOODMAN,
EDGAR SAMPSON and CHICK WEBB

Sax

Bright Swing

SUMMERTIME
from PORGY AND BESS®

SAX

Music and Lyrics by GEORGE GERSHWIN,
DuBOSE and DOROTHY HEYWARD
and IRA GERSHWIN

A TASTE OF HONEY

Words by RIC MARLOW
Music by BOBBY SCOTT

Sax

TEQUILA

SAX

By CHUCK RIO

UPTOWN FUNK

Sax

Words and Music by MARK RONSON,
BRUNO MARS, PHILIP LAWRENCE, JEFF BHASKER, DEVON GALLASPY,
NICHOLAUS WILLIAMS, LONNIE SIMMONS, RONNIE WILSON,
CHARLES WILSON, RUDOLPH TAYLOR and ROBERT WILSON

YAKETY SAX

SAX

Words and Music by JAMES RICH
and BOOTS RANDOLPH

Moderately, in 2

4th time, to Coda ⊕

HAL•LEONARD® SAXOPHONE PLAY-ALONG

The Saxophone Play-Along Series will help you play your favorite songs quickly and easily. Just follow the music, listen to the audio to hear how the saxophone should sound, and then play along using the separate backing tracks. Each song is printed twice in the book: once for alto and once for tenor saxes. The online audio is available for streaming or download using the unique code printed inside the book, and it includes **PLAYBACK+** options such as looping and tempo adjustments.

1. ROCK 'N' ROLL

Bony Moronie • Charlie Brown • Hand Clappin' • Honky Tonk (Parts 1 & 2) • I'm Walkin' • Lucille (You Won't Do Your Daddy's Will) • See You Later, Alligator • Shake, Rattle and Roll.

00113137 Book/Online Audio $16.99

2. R&B

Cleo's Mood • I Got a Woman • Pick up the Pieces • Respect • Shot Gun • Soul Finger • Soul Serenade • Unchain My Heart.

00113177 Book/Online Audio $16.99

3. CLASSIC ROCK

Baker Street • Deacon Blues • The Heart of Rock and Roll • Jazzman • Smooth Operator • Turn the Page • Who Can It Be Now? • Young Americans.

00113429 Book/Online Audio $16.99

4. SAX CLASSICS

Boulevard of Broken Dreams • Harlem Nocturne • Night Train • Peter Gunn • The Pink Panther • St. Thomas • Tequila • Yakety Sax.

00114393 Book/Online Audio. $16.99

5. CHARLIE PARKER

Billie's Bounce (Bill's Bounce) • Confirmation • Dewey Square • Donna Lee • Now's the Time • Ornithology • Scrapple from the Apple • Yardbird Suite.

00118286 Book/Online Audio $16.99

6. DAVE KOZ

All I See Is You • Can't Let You Go (The Sha La Song) • Emily • Honey-Dipped • Know You by Heart • Put the Top Down • Together Again • You Make Me Smile.

00118292 Book/Online Audio $16.99

7. GROVER WASHINGTON, JR.

East River Drive • Just the Two of Us • Let It Flow • Make Me a Memory (Sad Samba) • Mr. Magic • Take Five • Take Me There • Winelight.

00118293 Book/Online Audio $16.99

8. DAVID SANBORN

Anything You Want • Bang Bang • Chicago Song • Comin' Home Baby • The Dream • Hideaway • Slam • Straight to the Heart.

00125694 Book/Online Audio $16.99

9. CHRISTMAS

The Christmas Song (Chestnuts Roasting on an Open Fire) • Christmas Time Is Here • Count Your Blessings Instead of Sheep • Do You Hear What I Hear • Have Yourself a Merry Little Christmas • The Little Drummer Boy • White Christmas • Winter Wonderland.

00148170 Book/Online Audio $16.99

10. JOHN COLTRANE

Blue Train (Blue Trane) • Body and Soul • Central Park West • Cousin Mary • Giant Steps • Like Sonny (Simple Like) • My Favorite Things • Naima (Niema).

00193333 Book/Online Audio $16.99

11. JAZZ ICONS

Body and Soul • Con Alma • Oleo • Speak No Evil • Take Five • There Will Never Be Another You • Tune Up • Work Song.

00199296 Book/Online Audio $16.99

12. SMOOTH JAZZ

Bermuda Nights • Blue Water • Europa • Flirt • Love Is on the Way • Maputo • Songbird • Winelight.

00248670 Book/Online Audio $16.99

13. BONEY JAMES

Butter • Let It Go • Stone Groove • Stop, Look, Listen (To Your Heart) • Sweet Thing • Tick Tock • Total Experience • Vinyl.

00257186 Book/Online Audio $16.99

Prices, contents, and availability subject to change without notice.

Visit Hal Leonard online at **www.halleonard.com**